Plainsongs

Editor

Eric R. Tucker

Associate Editors

Becky Faber, Michael Catherwood, Eleanor Reeds

Editors Emeriti

Dwight Marsh, Laura Marvel-Wunderlich

Publisher

Corpus Callosum Press

Cover photo by Tricia Oman

Corpus Callosum Press
Hastings, Nebraska

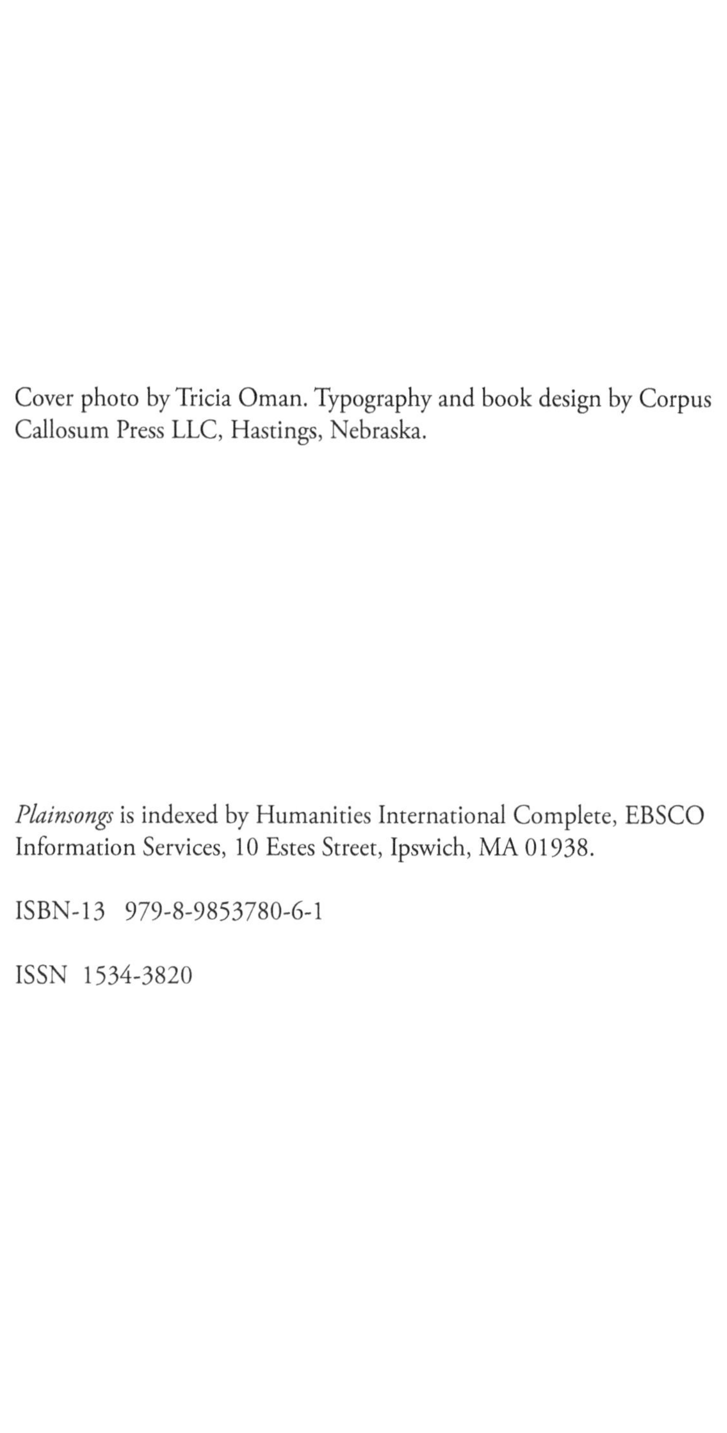

Cover photo by Tricia Oman. Typography and book design by Corpus Callosum Press LLC, Hastings, Nebraska.

Plainsongs is indexed by Humanities International Complete, EBSCO Information Services, 10 Estes Street, Ipswich, MA 01938.

ISBN-13   979-8-9853780-6-1

ISSN   1534-3820

Plainsongs

Winner of the Jane Geske Award,
presented by the Nebraska Center for the Book

Notes from the Editor

Thank you for picking up the latest issue of *Plainsongs*. The spring/summer 2023 issue features poems from over seventy contributing artists, including award-winning poems by Eric Chiles, Kerry Trautman, and Shauna Shiff. Inside you'll also find poetry by Nebraska state poet Matt Mason; *Plainsongs* associate editors Becky Faber, Michael Catherwood, and Eleanor Reeds; Omaha-based poet Kiara Nicole Letcher; and Eugene, Oregon–based writer Ulrick Casimir—all of whom will be reading their work live and in-person on the evening of April 1 at the Lark in Hastings, Nebraska. The event will be free and open to the public. If you're in the Hastings area on that night, why don't you come on by? We'd love to see you. And if you're currently reading this while sitting inside the Lark on April 1, I'm probably standing somewhere just over your shoulder. No, your other shoulder. Hey. Hi. Thanks for coming.

Plainsongs is now forty-three years old. That's a ripe old age for a literary journal these days. Over four decades. Seven years shy of fifty. Two score and three years. A mere 957 years short of a millennium. That's longer than the lifespans of both the average bison and the average pronghorn combined, and if you think a prairie dog can easily attain such an advanced age, then you clearly haven't spent three seconds googling the term *prairie dog lifespan*, as I have just now. A bit of online searching also reveals that in 1980, when *Plainsongs* came into being at Peru State College in Peru, Nebraska, the band Lipps Inc. reached No. 1 on the U.S. singles chart with their smash hit "Funkytown." Was the opening lyric—"gotta make a move to a town that's right for me"—the impetus for the momentous intrastate journey that *Plainsongs* was about to embark upon in the early 80s? Almost certainly not, but during those heady years, *Plainsongs* talked about, talked about, talked about movin' to Hastings College, and in 1983 it did just that. The energy must have been good there, because *Plainsongs* kept groovin' at Hastings College until 2020, when Corpus Callosum Press took the reins for a short while, and now, in the year 2023, the journal is heading back home to HC, which feels right.

Somehow, after roughly four average coyote lifespans, *Plainsongs* is still around. No, not *somehow*: *Plainsongs* is still around because of the vision and hard work of former editors Dwight Marsh and Laura Marvel Wunderlich and the dedication and perseverance of Becky,

Michael, Eleanor, and all the former readers and editors. They are the reason this journal is still here; *Plainsongs* would have disappeared years ago without their persistent efforts. They are the reason I have had the opportunity to be the editor of *Plainsongs* for the past eight years. And they are the reason the journal will continue to thrive for what I hope will be many more average elk lifespans to come.

It has been a great honor to be a part of this publication. Thank you for reading. Thank you for contributing your fine work. Thank you for purchasing. Thank you for supporting the arts and the humanities. Thank you for supporting Hastings College and HC Press, the new/old home of *Plainsongs*. Just: thank you.

Though I will no longer be the editor of *Plainsongs*, I will remain a fan for all time. If I'm lucky enough to still be groovin' on this planet an average grackle's lifespan from now, perhaps one day, while meandering through whatever iteration of the metaverse we're all plugged into, I'll happen upon a holographic advert for a live *Plainsongs* poetry event, to be held on the main stage at a fabulous venue somewhere in the vibrant heart of Funkytown. The VR interface will befuddle me, though, and the headset will worsen an already awful migraine, and after a few frantic midair swipes the *Plainsongs* ad will vanish and I'll find myself inexplicably standing beside my wife amid a vast digital expanse of wild Nebraska prairie. An avatar of a swift fox, whose lifespan is infinite, will scamper past; a simulacrum of sandhill cranes will glide overhead. Also, so many goddamn *wasps*— who felt the need to put wasps in the simulation? After searching for what feels like several average praying mantis lifespans, I'll discover a little wooden sign in the shape of an arrow, pointing the way to Funkytown. I'll wonder who might be in that timeless place, waiting. Our fathers, mothers, siblings, friends. All our lovely dogs. Perhaps those who helped nurture *Plainsongs* over the years: Laura and Dwight; Becky, Michael, and Eleanor; Tricia Oman; Ali Beheler; Steve Langan; Chris Goedert; Amy Sandeen; Antje Anderson; Mark Bauer; Robin Harrell; Turner McGehee; and so many others. In the distance, unmistakable bass thumps: Funkytown beckons. "Please," I'll whisper to my wife, as a spring wind howls across the Plains, sounding at times like protest, at times like laughter, at times like weeping, and always—*always*—like song, "won't you take me there?"

Eric R. Tucker
Hastings, Nebraska

Contents

Joe's whisper

In high school you were always quick
with a wise crack and a smile.
Without a care until
you lost your deferment because
you partied too much and flunked out.
Rather than wait for Uncle Sam to snap
you up, you signed up for Semper Fi.
I remember the night in Obee's garage
when you got back, all of us sipping beer.
There was a shadow in your smile,
things just didn't fit anymore
and late that night you told of us
of a search for Vietcong.
In a village you burst
through a hut's door
finding just a frightened woman
clutching a small child.
You froze.
Unsmiling you whispered
that the sergeant yanked you out
and tossed in a grenade.
The night's silence
exploded around us.

Eric Chiles
Bethlehem, Pennsylvania

About "Joe's Whisper": A Plainsongs Award Poem

I have known "Joe"—and many of his brothers. I remember the Draft and its correlation to education deferments. I saw my male friends and relatives head off to Basic Training, then later deploy to Vietnam. I attended their going-away parties, cried at their funerals, and sipped beer with those who returned. All of this is to say that "Joe's Whisper" has a deep context for me.

On July 3, 1971—in the midst of the Vietnam conflict—William Stafford wrote his morning journal thought: *Every war has two losers.*

Only two? No. The poet has given us a view of the wider result. The happy-go-lucky All-American Joe of the early lines joins the Marines in line 7. The use of second person builds the bond—<u>you</u> and <u>I</u>—that begins to develop in line 8. The pronouns become an essential part of this ripple effect to build to the last word of the poem—<u>us</u>—where the sergeant's action, as told through Joe, expands the reaction.

The pebble-in-the-water effect of that grenade is solidly developed: the impact on the woman and child; the impact on Joe; the impact on the listener/narrator; and at the end an impact on the reader. Neal Shusterman wrote, "When you drop a pebble into a pond, ripples spread out changing all the water in the pool. …the pond is never the same again." "Joe's Whisper" is a pebble in the pond of both the narrator's experience as well as in our national experience.

While this poem is powerful on its own, it would be a strong companion piece for those who teach/read Bobbie Ann Mason's *In Country* or Tim O'Brien's *The Things They Carry*.

Becky Faber
Lincoln, Nebraska

Practice

Never in school did I
crouch under the desk, quiet, quiet.
But my children do.
Fold their skinny limbs into a tight
origami shape
and are instructed to stay still.
Shh, they are told,
pretend there is a boy
stalking the hall. He looks like a boy
but he is a wolf hunting.
He looks like any boy you know
but do not trust him.
He has a taste now for small children.
When the door rattles because
the boy wants in, the teacher
warns with a look.
No recess if you make a noise.
My children want recess,
they want what all children want
to return home
to their mothers
so they bury their heads
into the square bone of their knees.
and wait to see
if this time it is just a drill.

Shauna Shiff
Warrenton, Virginia

About "Practice": A Plainsongs Award Poem

In the 1960s in grade school, during the Cold War, about once a month, we practiced nuclear attack drills. There were air-raid shelters, monthly air-raid sirens, sonic booms from jets stationed at Offutt Air Base. It was all a little spooky and alarming. In Shauna Shiff's poem "Practice," the reader finds a new tension, a new horror. Shiff weaves together an understated poem that carries great weight with a razor focus on a current, almost daily, terror.

Shiff begins "Practice" gently: "Never in school did I / crouch under the desk, quiet, quiet." Children in the poem "Fold their skinny limbs into a tight / origami shape." The tone of the poem engages silence, and playful language, both techniques teachers use so children are not alarmed.

The difference between what these children are practicing and what we practiced in the 60s is that children now have, almost daily, examples of school shootings. The terror continues like an avalanche, undeterred by hopeful "thoughts and prayers." And there's fallout from preparation and drills, for parents and children. We are damaged by unrelenting feelings of threats, by our government's inability to act to protect citizens. But that's another matter. Or is it? A strong poem presents questions. "Practice" quietly presents a terror our country continues to suffer.

The poem continues and builds on the wolf theme where the wolf looks like a "boy" and is "wolf hunting." Shiff continues with the understated imagery: "When the door rattles because / the boy wants in," and the story of the intruder continues. The teacher warns, "No recess if you make a noise." The children do as told, "so they bury their heads / into the square bone of their knees."

Shiff's poem explores the anxiety and quiet fear we all feel with children's "Practice" of shooting drills. Shiff ends her poem as the children "wait to see / if this time it is just a drill." The final line paralyzes us all.

Michael Catherwood
Omaha, Nebraska

A Drowning Person Doesn't Always Look Like Drowning

The polio survivor in the iron
lung knows how few technicians there are

to repair such machines. How can a man
sleep with airflow vulnerable to snapped

bolts and power grids? Everything can rupture
under the right burden—even femurs
or railroad bridges. Weaknesses splintered-into—

like all the awful things we save up
to say to people we love in just

the right fight moment. These lungs
I choke with are the same sacs that once

filled themselves with my mother's fluid.
Clavicles and ribs that crack can't be

fiberglassed into casts, rather the body around
them must agree to rest the muscles bent on

tugging those bones around. Let this be apology
to the bones of my ten-year-old self for having

grown old, having stretched them thin like
pulled taffy, having loaded them with weight

of sorrow and cake. Someone invented
the motorized rotating bed

my father's comatose body was strapped into
like a pickup-truck bed of lumber, tilting

his mass left or right every other hour
to keep fluid from tidepooling his lungs. How

can a woman sleep knowing all the songs
she's stopped her lungs singing? Imagine

your ribcage made of brass, and how
many birds could rest safely inside, and how

their songs could echo out of your mouth
opened like the lid of music box. My father

awoke from his coma to tv helicopter
footage of New Orleans submerged

by Hurricane Katrina. *What country is this?*
Apology to the lungs I douse with

housepaint fumes, pork smoke, and
daiquiri-scent candles. Everything hidden

inside that we rely upon to shape
and inflate us will someday fail,

overwhelmed by what's been asked of it
by its DNA, by a self-important brain. Imagine

an endless supply of tools, so many ways to not
need them, ways to not need anyone.

Kerry Trautman
Findlay, Ohio

About "A Drowning Person Doesn't Always Look Like Drowning": A Plainsongs Award Poem

From the opening image of the polio survivor dependent upon an obsolete relic of medical technology, Kerry Trautman reminds her readers that our very breath is contingent upon the most fragile of foundations. She asks us how such a man could "sleep with airflow vulnerable to snapped / bolts and power grids," marvelling at the ability to rest easily under such a threat. While the poem continuously emphasizes the physicality and thus the breakability of the human body, it also acknowledges our susceptibility to other less tangible forms of wounding such as "all the awful things we save up / to say to people we love." When a second rhetorical question about someone's sleep is posed, it is the "songs / she's stopped her lungs singing" that are considered an unbearable menace thwarting a woman's peace.

This poem asks us twice how one can succumb to unconsciousness, willingly become more defenseless. It also tells us twice why our fear is both assumed and assured."Everything can rupture / under the right burden." "Everything hidden // inside that we rely upon to shape / and inflate us will someday fail." These statements identify weakness as universal and defeat as certain. While humans persist in inventing life-saving devices and fathers may wake up from comas, we must still face our inability to repair a broken rib and to insulate our apparently civilized lives from natural disasters.

This poem commands us twice: "Imagine." Both imperatives come before a stanza break and then Trautman unfolds an impossible scene of security. Rather than not only breakable but also unfixable bones "stretched … thin like / pulled taffy," "your ribcage" might instead be "made of brass" and thus become a space for birds to "rest safely" and sing. Rather than relying on existing natural and manmade structures, the "femurs" and "railroad bridges" that can shatter, we might instead have "an endless supply of tools" or discover "so many ways to not / need them." Here, of course, Trautman's ethics comes into focus as the poem ends by demonstrating that the ultimate goal of such fantasies of strength is very far from desirable. Despite all our fears, we should not want to live in a world in which we have found "ways not to need anyone."

Eleanor Reeds
Hastings, Nebraska

Blind Spot

He loves the sound of her voice,
the soft tone as well as the fluency of her words—
like a river that moves at a natural rate.

She loves his focus,
how he pays attention to each word,
using his ears to carry the load
that his eyes no longer can.

Perhaps they should have met earlier,
but their stars did not cross until now
in this quiet spot in the Veterans Hospital
for a short time each week.

After these sessions
he carries the sound of her words
as tightly as his rifle in the jungle,
her words smoother than the Mekong River ever was.

He wants to ask her what she was like at 18,
but he fears that she will ask him the same question.

He doesn't want to talk about that.
He doesn't want to explain about the Green-Water Navy.

He is afraid that he would tell her too much.
Even useless eyes can cry.

Becky Faber
Lincoln, Nebraska

Daddy's Girl

I suppose that I was four,
big enough to go outside by myself
but not strong enough to help myself
when my shoes became stuck in the mud.
I wailed loudly, drawing my father from the barn
to come pick me up and carry me to the house.

He never walked me down the aisle.
I robbed him of that. His oldest daughter,
I eloped, leaving a note on the kitchen table telling him
what I had done. We never spoke of it.

A wretched daughter either wises up
or continues to be wretched. I chose
the former.

At ninety he was failing,
could not walk on his own.
I took him out on a spring day,
pushing his wheelchair while
making small talk. On the edge of the sidewalk
we found a nickel. I picked it up and
put it in his hand. His fingers had grown soft.
I wanted to keep pushing the wheelchair
to any place other than where he was headed.

Becky Faber
Lincoln, Nebraska

Home Movie (8 mm)

The yellow light seeps in
behind the garage and a dull
thumb blotches the lens.
There's a rub of red paint
along the window; a glide
swing rusts against the fence.

The neighbor's house
gleams and vibrates in
the background and Grandfather
waits by the back door.

The film reveals few clues.
The backyard fireplace
crumbles into the earth
and the camera quickly pans away.
The image then swings to the sky
where a jet holds and stitches
contrails through clouds.

Now, Grandfather waves
his large hand goodbye.
The camera holds
for a long awkward
moment on an empty
doorway. His world here
began in New York
in 1901 where as an infant he
came from Hungary,
no cameras or jets, the future
both darkness and promise.

Michael Catherwood
Omaha, Nebraska

Perhaps Optimism

sings under the wing
that cuts the air and clouds
to shreds; ethereal
droplets are old show tunes.

We cannot see heavens
where the blue lightens
but feel the cold stares
of evening stars beginning.

Below, farms and streets
lose their tragedy where a child
looks upward into the sky.
There is Pocatello, perhaps

Boise, now a mountain,
moving across the suspension
of color and water
and light. Farms below

are squares of beauty.
The work unseen
from here. The child
loses us in the clouds.

Michael Catherwood
Omaha, Nebraska

The Beach That Came Back

In Ireland, there was a beach
That came back. The sand all washed away
30 years ago, but one night, a freak storm
Covered up the craggy rocks again.
Was it the Sea of Faith that Arnold saw
Retreating at Dover now come back
Like a rough beast slouching toward
The coast of County Mayo?
The house prices went back up.
The tourist board were thrilled.
On Achill Island, the waiting
Paid off. Toes sank into yellow sand
Once more; the callouses were burnished
Off, developed after too many walks
With stone felt beneath a cork sole.
The sea level's rising, we can't go back,
The glaciers will all have melted
To submerge so many isles.
But a beach came back, like love,
Like faith, like hope, like waiting
For a summer of one's youth spent
In peaty rain, with soda bread and fiddling,
MySpace breaks and childhood ending.
A beach came back. A beach came back.

Eleanor Reeds
Hastings, Nebraska

After Ever After

Marriage, of course, and children —

does Belle struggle to teach her feral brood
how to read, play chess? what if their father,
however handsome and polished now,
perfected the roar and scares them?
her sisters are statues so the children
become fond of them in characteristic ways,
discovering and reaffirming the magic of transformation
through, if not love, need and gratitude.

does Sleeping Beauty risk a christening?
does she take up tapestry and weaving
and needlework and never want to nap?
or was her gift patience, self-care, priorities
that frustrate so many in their spouse?

I imagine Snow White never cleaning,
afraid of child-size chairs and crockery,
fearful that her boys will never become
more than stunted men, her girls more
than objects in a glass box. suspicious
of mirrors and vanity, even her own fairness.

does Bluebeard's wife remarry? does she,
a blue streak in her hair, dare to become
a husband killer too? a femme fatale,
prying into great men's secrets,
a necklace heavy with blood red keys.

Eleanor Reeds
Hastings, Nebraska

9 of Swords

The air overheard is crisp
the sky covered in haze
someone is burning fall foliage
and dead summer grass

Last night I dreamt that I couldn't stop bleeding
last night I dreamt that I couldn't stop running
legs aching of acid

Snapshots and sticky notes to remember
your fantasies or disruptions

Notes on anger: A void or a dense forest
mind in blooms and vines

Photos on want: Mouth always open in laughter
or a tearing cry ripped open
some busted lip

Notes on beauty: A bouquet of red roses
layers of petals
rich luxuriant soil
a peony bush glimmering in a back yard

Moths pour into the streetlight
pull open a dream unsnap the buttons of its shirt
put hands into its chest
prize it open to show a 9 sword heart
my head in my hands again

I read that sometimes falling in love is much less
glamorous than it appears on TV

Butterfly into moth & butterfly into moth

I have many notes on transformation
but they all contradict themselves.

Kiara Nicole Letcher
Omaha, Nebraska

You cannot scrub me out

I am a blood stain
cheap Merlot headache pain

Hang on while my voice whispers like
steam and mist phantoming from a lake
rising up like hair standing on end

Nonsymmetrical and fearful
I don't think I have much grace left
I have boiled my linens and washed my anger
hung them on a clothesline

Weeping in my Sunday best
there is no time for softness.

Kiara Nicole Letcher
Omaha, Nebraska

There Is a Turtle Crossing Highway 20

As you approach it,
you see it
as rubbish, a strip
from a tire, some black shape,
  you start to suspect
  it's moving, though,
  as you speed closer,

you squint your eyes and,
  yes, it's moving,
but how fast, you wonder,
seeing a car in the distance
coming this way
in the lane the thing moves
toward the shoulder of,

  in the flick of time
  you whip past it,
  you see this
  is no aquarium pet,
  this

is a goddamn dinosaur,
spiked tail, ancient hatchet-beak, you
know it will make it,
it clearly has
a million times before.

Matt Mason
Omaha, Nebraska

September 11, 2021

The morning light stays soft deep
into the day, it feels
like a movie, a love story,
not filtered by wildfires a thousand miles away,

my wife
sits on the bed,
bends to take our dog's face in her hands
while our daughters

bump breakfasts together,
stumble into rough plans;
none of it
was supposed to be here,

we weren't meant to happen
like this,
riding
on a rock
humming faster than we can figure
in cold
and dark
and emptiness,

such warmth,
such light,
so much.

Matt Mason
Omaha, Nebraska

Parting Shot

when silence comes
leaves twitch
and we wait

where the moon bleaches fabric
the light should fall across our bed
and be our very first spark

when passion won't come in the dark:
leaves blow
and we wait

Ulrick Casimir
Eugene, Oregon

Never Have I Ever

Never never post things on Twitter that Izzy Gutierrez might ever read. Never bet more than a hundred bucks on a game of straight pool. Never date my ex-girlfriend; never leave a dog in a car with the windows up on a hot summer day. And never—ever—let her see you sweat.

Never don't stop 'til you get (enough). Never tell a lie when the truth will do, except in those instances when boldfaced utter prevarication would clearly do just as well. Never be afraid to look a girl in her middle eye and call it quits. Never stop reading a book in the middle, and if painting is your thing, never try digesting more than a single double-length triptych at a time. Never say no, no, no to rehab—start smoking and if you do, please don't never stop.

Never stare at the sun: never sin at the store. Never snore no more, unless it's painful. Never sigh at a woman unless she's prayerful. Never tell a girl you love her until it's almost too late. Never propose marriage on your first ever date. And never, ever, let 'em see you sweat.

Never do the things you never said you were going to do when you turned thirteen. Never action Jackson—never doubt Bo Jackson. And never bet more than ten dollars on a single rack of straight pool.

Never let her listen to Chris Isaak on a rainy day—in fact, never let her listen to Chris Isaak at all (she'll get ideas). Speaking of: Never listen to a single smart thing your mother ever said, never. Never let autocorrect change "thung" when you meant "thing" to "thong"—in texts to said mother, results may be disappointing. Never think that when your woman says yes once, she is actually saying yes more than just that one goddamned time. Because you should never confuse reality with the truth, just like you should never argue with an arguer: It's like donating fresh and bleeding chunks of your own flesh-colored time.

Never give up on your most important muscle, the heart.

Ulrick Casimir
Eugene, Oregon

Still Life

All these buildings
Stand with open
Mouths to taste

The orange
I peel thinking
Of the Ponderosa

Pines I'm gathered in.
All those
Needles,

Lost in name,
Bearing the weight
Of still air. When

A pine is planted,
We call it autumn.
I plant flowers

For no other reason
Than to sing.
I want that

Clove-like aroma
To fill me.
Did I grasp

For the throat
Of the lily
As though there were still time?

Tyler Michael Jacobs
Bowling Green, Ohio

African Violets

We find them between the ties of hushed rails,
        or cracked school yard blacktops,
even between control joints of sidewalks
        that bank an abandoned city street,
the discarded things of human hand,
        the undesired, uprooted, burnt
by controlled flame, or shorn
        against summer dust.

Midwest yards harbor them,
        delicate, beautiful,
as if heaven, filled with stars,
        scattered across zoysia,
a cloudless sky in negative,
        the grass, endless space,
the blooms, darkened stars,
        and we, angels in our glory.

Their persistence is what frightens me,
        cultivated, urbane, refined,
righting words in straight furrows
        as if orderliness, being in itself,
gives rise against nature's ordered chaos,
        takes root in the measured gardens,
earth turned under plow,
        each spring planting given to its fall.

Yet, I love them so much.
        Those things we name weeds,
in their uncommon plainness,
        unplanned, unintended,
comfort me in deep-rooted knowing
        that after the plotting, and platting,
the unconceived, the un-engendered,
        will cover our feral desire.

Richard Stimac
Maplewood, Missouri

The Drive-Through Line to Nowhere

isn't moving,
as if you'd inched
out of your life
into a tableau,
the speakers in each lane
emitting static in bursts
yet endlessly voiceless,
the exhaust from the SUV
in front of you—
the one that took cuts,
imposing its Nietzschean will
on all the little Corollas
by its gargantuan bulk—
spewing a noxious
though invisible cloud
that would instantly gag you
if you rolled down
your driver's window,
while out on the street
cars are zooming by,
swishing a breeze your way
as if in mockery,
and you realize
any endless circle
in Dante's Inferno
would be preferable
to the hell
of not being able
to back up or roll forward,
of eternally occupying
this exact spot
like a butterfly
encased in amber,
its wings unfurled
but forever flightless.

Patricia L. Hamilton
Jackson, Tennessee

Field Hands

Open fields
tell the story
of renewal. Hands

make life,
moment to moment,
as August days

slow-travel
toward tomorrows.
With work, regular,

routine, focused,
memory slips
into open furrows.

God made hands
to be outdoors,
free, not cuffed,

nor clasped
in church
reaching for grace.

Hands are honest.
Committed to work
in open fields, they

hold no secrets,
have no need
to speak.

Nancy Cook
Saint Paul, Minnesota

156 Stewart Street

Vacated for sale.
A house built by my grandfather's rough, proud hands;
six decades of polishing appliances—the stove, the Frigidaire—
filling little knicks with white porcelain glaze
and Depression-era care.
Brass doorknobs worn by years of use,
copper cabinet detail with spades pointing up and down,
in my grandparents' ghost town.
The main level's low-ceiling stucco arches
leading from empty room to room.
Sweltering attic bedrooms with hidden panel closets
filled with metal hanger spacers.
Pink!
Pink kitchen tile, pink toilet;
pink formica, chrome-trimmed milkshake counter.
Curves,
     and angles.
Curves from the copper waves of the Nutone range hood
to the ornate swirls on the 1, 5, and 6 screwed onto the gray siding.
Angles from the dovetails to the hardwood door frames,
to the square bottle glass windows on the lower level.
Atomic doors with diamonds stepping down the wooden door.
Cinder blocks cooling the cellar all summer.
Garage no longer packed full.
Exhausted awnings and
a long, sad shadow cast through the iron porch rail.

Kari Martindale
Ijamsville, Maryland

Junk Drawer

Buried in the junk drawer
under strata of memories
pencil nubs bottle caps
spare buttons batteries
watch band links stamps
matchbooks orphaned keys
rusty pliers rubber bands
poker chips tweezers
safety pins thumb tacks
paper clips screwdrivers
broken birthday candles
pens and empty lighters
a little plastic triceratops
emerges from childhood past
scuffed but uncompressed
by the weight of time.

Ryan Nelson
Lincoln, Nebraska

Lizard

The lizard in me has been keeping still,
blending into the background of my life:
the house, the get-togethers,
the nightly meals and nightly Netflix—
all of it flickering across my line of vision,
taking it in for what it might mean
or letting it move across and through me,
sliding off my lizard back
where I can flick it safely away.

For long stretches of time,
it may seem I am not moving.
I love the heat I can lie in.
I love the crack between the wall
and floor which I can slide into
like a letter in an envelope,
the message there but unsent.
How good just to lie and be,
content with my lizard life,
taking in the world through
the scales of my skin, my tongue,
and my remarkable, parietal eye.

Lucy Adkins
Lincoln, Nebraska

Hour of the Bat

Hour of pale summer light, thick air
　　　teeming with mosquito and gnat,
　　　　　descending toward earth's warm ear.

Hour of cocktails, toothpicks flung
　　　about carelessly, Scotch smooth, neat.
　　　　　Hour of electric surrender.

Hour of trees fading into dark,
　　　relief of leaf and branch gone. Hour
　　　　　of blurred clouds, unsettled horizons.

Hour of clamor in the roost,
　　　a restless mammalian hunger.
　　　　　Hour of dim, wakeful, anxious cries.

Hour of eventide to night,
　　　exodus falls from cave, bridge, hollow
　　　　　tree, lifts en masse. Hour of wings.

Hour of pulse and echo, springed
　　　touch, hurried syllables of clasp
　　　　　and snare. Hour of mad unrest.

Hour of light-boned, terrestrial
　　　flyers, swarming, sweeping, pursuing
　　　　　what we cannot and will not see.

Amy Spade
Oakland, California

the terrier confessional

he limps from his tiny bed
to join me in early morning hours

lies at my feet and listens to misery
attempting escape—a ghost the quiet accepts

my dog does not judge—he associates
feels the fibrous membrane

of field briars growing thick within me
he stands guard like Cerberus

and comes closest when I resurrect
the dead—knows my feet

need his warmth

Terry Jude Miller
Richmond, Texas

Ghazal: With the Dead

after Rafael Campo

We know there is no being through with the dead,
our memory unfettered canvas we imbue with the dead.

Snow bares us its bones while Caity rehearses the eulogy. My mother
cradles her grief, a flame she flickers into with the dead.

Floral arrangements swell, deliver us from darker places. I watch
the circus roses, their wilting a fate I see through with the dead.

The worst things I've seen—fresh bananas, gallon of milk unopened,
telephone off the hook—I strain to undo with the dead.

On the floor of my apartment, I follow the waning sunlight with
my body but not my eyes, a tenderness I pursue with the dead.

When this is all over, we told one another, *we'll love better than ever
    before.*
But when the whole world died, nobody knew what to do with the
    dead.

In the plains, we know wind like terror. I lie in tall grass, certain
    only of
what brushes my cheek. A memory, a stillness: you, with the dead.

Sydney Vance
Edmond, Oklahoma

Anatomy of a Broadleaf Shark

You balk every time I jump, faint
Eeks slipping from my chapped lips
      But you can't bring yourself to swim
      In open waters for fear of sharks even
When fresh.

We used to run
On hard streets, carried like seeds
      Of dandelions, wispy white bombs
      Flying silently through their flower
Beds, laying claim of soft dirt.

You thought
I flew as fast as you, but I was afraid
      To let go of the stalk keeping me
      Grounded, all taproots and toothy
Leaves. And when I confessed to you
Fertilizer pumped into shrunken veins
      Chumming your confidence like the
      Imaginary fish used to distract your
prey.

Rebecca Thrush
Charlton, Massachusetts

Scrap Yard

Another vision, vaulted, ad hoc
(Whatever this time it may have been)
Was asked to bear too much
And then, quickly or not, was given up on,
Left for shrapnel that sags and bends
Ribless back and forth, asunder—metallic
Scribbling in a distant, rustic corner
Like a molecule drawn on screen
But lacking legend or locant.

Within, a mouse with bead-drop eyes
Has claimed its canopy and peacefully
Broods over a rosehip cache. A sparrow
In the ease of no one watching
Weaves in and out of the mangle,

Building nest while the other sings,
Rattling what's left of the core, a pulse
In the throat that sends accipiter
Leaning, nodding to the musical turn
Pausing—listening—
As if someone had once been thinking
There is safety in singing
And in being heard.

Adrian Williams
Burlington, Vermont

Rimbaud's Electric Guitar

she comes on big cat haunches
to abide in the purple blood
      somewhere between red and blue.
      limping, not completely dead, but needy.
an electric-purple-glowing-sunburst-renaissance
pleading for hands
      to stroke her strings.
         someone with uncombed hair and
an ongoing story lifts her.

turning big clear eyes,
she studies the room in her reflection.

she takes what's in the air
and makes you feel
something

reassuring
      as
      her vibrations / singing throat
vibrations combine with
delicate attention
in a oneness of melody.
she's whatever we've
  wept for
threaded in rhythm.
counsel that stirs
a drastic healing element.
a restoration of faith because
these words plunge headfirst
      for the heart.

i follow a wavy line into the spirit
world,
and you, oh my soul
are this guitar, me.
      sounding more fragrant by the year
discipline, singularity of vision,

right brain expression,
a grunting murmur
as a stray leg swipes
me on the way to the bathroom
        at night.
a family jamboree.
        to be played beautifully
        makes us more
        than we've ever, ever been
all these things are me, of me.
impossible is possible
if you agree.
lunch is dinner
for the bees.

Daniel Alexander Barry
Phoenixville, Pennsylvania

Driving to Visit Family We See a Tipped-Over Freight Engine

Immediately I think of those truly massive herbivores
eons extinct. Sauropod or ceratopsian.
If one gave up grazing mid-prairie and folded
to history's icy embrace. I nearly say

Was that always there? Suddenly I can't bring to bear
this familiar strip of land without the exposed
undercarriage of rods and wheels, the day's heat lifting off
those inner workings like a grill. Funny how
fast the mind makes its adjustment. A switch

flips. This rambling, hissing, endeavoring
machine now embodies stagnancy.
Isn't that also what happened to the country?
One second it's *feu de joie* and home-sewn flags.
The next, personhood for thousands is slashed by two-fifths.

The train isn't gone, but its trainness is.
The potential within its suit of metal dissolved
like a rumor. It can't be the thing it's dressed as,
so what is it?
I need a way of talking about this not-train train

like I need a way of talking about not-America
America wherein geriatric white men own
my uterus, and migrant children are treated like bulk
goods with pesky storage needs.
What do you call a thing that's just

a thing, and not also the idea of it? What do you call
flesh the earth refuses to take back, that rots and
rots and never wastes away, that the sun splits
open at every seam, pours in, but doesn't purify?
Maybe someday a name will come to me.

But don't let it be today.
Today all I want is to drive to see my nieces:
Three exuberant sisters, each with a new, urgent story
spilling from her lips like tokens, like slot machine winnings
overflowing my big-ass souvenir cup.

Amy O'Reilly
Webster Groves, Missouri

"Skull with its Lyric Appendage Leaning on a Night Table Which Should Have the Exact Temperature of a Cardinal Bird's Nest" (Dali, 1934)

We do not know what happens now.
If we tried to say, it might diminish us
like an explanation of a bird pecking
at the last kernels in the bottom
of a sack of empty popcorn.
There must have been a funny clown here
minutes before, a carousel, children,
we say, though that too diminishes us.
We have been diminished before
and lived to tell, but this time it seems
different, this time it truly diminishes us.
Say it: we have not come all this way
to be diminished, though still we
do not know now what happens.
We are here, it seems to be victorious:
a bird pecking at the last kernels
in the bottom of a sack of empty popcorn,
a bird who doesn't know where
any of this will lead, if anywhere,
whether there will be another sky
in which ever to fly again, whether
his new weight will afford him that sky.

Paul Dickey
Omaha, Nebraska

Nobody does.

There are a few things I should tell you about the Cowboy Soul
because a lot of people get it wrong.
It's not what you see on television, and it's not about boys.
It does live in the West, but it lives in other places too.

The Cowboy Soul wears very red lipstick,
which it leaves behind in little kisses on its cigarette butts.
Every night it sleeps under the stars,
but the stars don't own the Cowboy Soul,
nobody does.

And I wish I had better news for you but
the Cowboy Soul is a fucking forest fire.
And I do mean a hysterical force of nature beyond human dignity
    or shame.
It thinks nothing of you, owes nothing to you, and cannot
    be venged.

But it hasn't been all cake for the Cowboy Soul either.
The Cowboy Soul spends its whole life longing.
In fact, the time it spends longing is much longer than the time it
    longs for.
And that's a lot longer than you.

Stephanie Young
Denver, Colorado

First Day of Hunting Season

We're here for Beth to be offered
a position at the local university.
Someone in the department
lends us a car and swears
the state park is great for hiking,
but fails to mention this is the first
day of hunting season, more guns
than at the Somme or on D-Day,
so I wonder how sincere
they are about Beth coming here.

The woods may indeed be,
"lovely, dark and deep,"
but we won't be walking
in them today: too many
trigger-happy hunters
so desperate to bag a trophy buck,
they'll shoot at any noise, any
wind-lifted movement: too many
kids shot off puttering scooters.

Instead, we'll walk quaint streets,
sink into the bookstore's arm chairs,
read peacefully in the coffee bar,
before dinner at the dean's house,
while now we wipe cappuccino foam,
not blood, from our upper lips.

Robert Cooperman
Denver, Colorado

Bog Pond

He knew the things that move the fastest
were the first to die
so he waited each night as dark slipped forward
like the slowest law handed down from
the highest peak,
refused to tremble
as dark oozed
over the horizon, hung there like
an end of him—
a boy who searched each day for nothing
and was sure to never find it
under the sun or under the moon
where he learned to keep himself calm
by sharpening flint heads
on a fist-sized granite
he wouldn't trade
for a god or a gun.

Long after the sun left
the wind blew down low
before rising to lull over the thick black settle
lying heavy across the bog pond,
luring the agile groundhogs and woodchucks
down the dank hill to where the creek
gave up the ghost.
He watched the animals run to the dark water
and bound from the bank and sink
out of sight in the bog turned black
by all the nights that came to it
from all over
and fell down dead.

John Riley
Greensboro, North Carolina

I've created a thing that will never bring me pleasure

Birds claw the remnant of its brain.

I study the minutes.

Click by. I am asking the question

how will I have the time. Those small sturdy bones

snap in my feet. Men repair on the scaffolding.

I do not want my face

carved into rock. I do not want to be remembered. Wind buffets

the ice floes. The north. The east. Disintegrate as leaving

the belly of the earth. Coded myself

fat and a liquid. Equivocate. Equivocate. Planets in see. Corpses

bottom ocean and river. Muted hocks of light. Children pop

out of mother. I couldn't bottom

the thrust on my heart, I couldn't be

ghost nor familiar.

Margaret Saigh
Pittsburgh, Pennsylvania

Marriage

if simplicity is defined
as a single moment
stripped down to a blurry
amber-hued Polaroid
the images captured in mid-intent
like chess pieces
riding the territorial divide
between dark and light

and complexity holds its ground
within the quarrel of sparrows
nests in shambles and
the taste of honeydew after a funeral

my stance remains a mystery
while I sit at our table
with two salt shakers
and a bowl of persimmons

staring out the window
waiting for you to come home

Lynn Fuller
Evanston, Illinois

Jersey City Nocturne

Too soon to call it a ruin,
this gap between the tenements
that I once called home.
No room here for nostalgia,
but there are lingering echoes
for those inclined to listen.

Here, where ivy threads its leaves
through a chain link fence,
stood a white brick building
with wrought iron gates
that might have appeared graceful
in some other setting.

Children played dizzying games of tag,
relishing the freedom of summer,
and debating the encroaching darkness
with pin-curled mothers in housedresses
who appeared on the stoops like town-criers
announcing the arrival of evening.

Time's passage on this street
is measured only by decay.
But there is a melody here
in the glow of the streetlight
where I listen to the urban nocturne
of weeds rustling in a vacant lot.

Gloria Heffernan
Syracuse, New York

Sunday Morning

I read Margaret Atwood
writing about wolves
on a hard chair in the kitchen.

I put my curly messy
hair up in an elastic band.
I'm in yesterday's unzipped

jeans, the bra I wore
to bed. I dreamt about my favorite

forest, now fenced off, forbidden.
Stay in your yard. Don't get too wild.
Danger, danger. Girls alone. Watch out.

Erica and I walked through
those clumps of trees
and dirt, following the foot

path we tread by heart to Giant
Eagle where we bought Hostess
Pudding Pies, 5 cent candies.

Awake, I drink old, reheated coffee
from a dog mug, miss my free roaming

childhood.

In dreams, we wander the woods,
swing on vines, wade in creek water,
and we both still live in Pittsburgh.

Lori D'Angelo
Mount Solon, Virginia

A Drowned Man's Search for Meaning

Some days
the harbormaster, the bookkeeper
the editor-in-chief, the umpire
agree to meet
(as assigned)
in a quiet café
in Barcelona
or on a hill
on the coast
just east of San Sebastian.

Those dissolving cafés.

Such cafés with
tables under trees,
a bowl of oranges
and warm bread in the shade.

They are given mint
tea, with lots of sugar.
They stay quiet.
Smiling like Mona Lisa
at each other, relieved
to take time off.

They are not distracted
but still they don't comment
on the sandpiper
on the beach below
who's let go
of the ideas
causing its pains.
Without them
the sandpiper finds
amethyst in
the universal grains,
with or
without worry.

Some days the octopus
needs no ink.

HR Harper
Felton, California

Principal

My brothers and I saw a lot of my father,
more than most kids did.
We saw him at breakfast,
his countenance already structured
for the school day ahead.
We saw him on and off all day,
striding down halls,
breaking up trysts at the lockers,
popping into classrooms unannounced—
also his disembodied,
loudspeakered voice
announcing this and that.
Weekends too,
directing chores on Saturday,
and of course church services, twice, on Sunday.
He ate supper with us and Mom,
although we seldom saw him in the evenings.
He was always at school board,
choir practice, prayer meeting,
or speaking to the Mothers Club.

Yet, for all that, the only times
we really met him were those
several summers at the cabin,
our mutual escape,
when righteousness was left on the prairie
in favor of gardening and cookouts
and, for a hour or so each afternoon,
playing Sorry and Clue with his sons….

And the only way I can tolerate
this dry, dogmatic funeral
in this dead-aired church
is to remember shucking his corn and shelling his peas,
and him, aproned, laughing with us under the pines,
grilling wieners for his family.

Jim Krosschell
Newton Highlands, Massachusetts

To my single chin hair, with tweezers in hand

More often these days, I find my fingers absent-
mindedly grazing near your epidermic quarters,
nails brushing the thin beginnings of your body
which is also, of course, my body.
Over two decades, you made yourself
comfortable in the crescent of my chin, your crest
stitched in skin since I was made
airborne by accident by my brother
then five and hugging me
too close to the bookshelf, letting go
too soon and leaving me behind
a wound which ages
later we discover never fully
closed.

Elusive bitch, you are
there and then you are not
never enough to notice until you are
long enough
to be
detached.
Oh sweetie
stop trembling, you knew
from the start this was going to happen.
Your killer was named before you
even began to read
this poem. This will only hurt
a little, at first, and then
we can talk again
later when you've grown
again, just enough
to be a bother
just below the brink
of me.

Riley O'Connell
San Mateo, California

High Gravity Days (A Poem for Myself)

*in a weird way I'm afraid of being afraid to fall, because I really don't want to
have fear.*
    —Vertical Addiction, Mountain Project climbing forum

you want to blame the moon
for high gravity days   when weight
feels persuasive   you want to climb
but your feet never leave the ground
        you blame performance on the earth
feeling tighter   but those claustrophobic days
are becoming more frequent
than they are not
it cannot *just* be the earth keeping you
            down

high gravity days really
sounds like an excuse for being afraid
        of falling
sounds like a metaphor for all the other
        things you fear

what happened   when did you become this way

you grew up racing horses without tack
bounding through the trees   but
now just the thought of weight and hooves
and hooves and hooves and hooves

        at 24
every day feels like the heaviest one yet

perhaps because you are afraid of the day
your father will pass   and nothing
can make up for those years
you couldn't part your lips to tell him
you love him   nothing can

and your mother too   despite
immortal hour-long phone calls
every other day   just checking in
to hear the tongue of the home
body that raised you

and you don't even want to think
about your brothers

your lover

the gravity
gets heavier

and you want to believe in reincarnation
but you're too afraid of God

and you want so badly to believe that the
ticks on a clock can be recycled

yet you waste your time writing
and deleting lines of a poem
that will never escape the shackles
of the page   never witness the sun
traverse the sky

and meanwhile there's an unread note
that your father wrote for you
when you left home for the first time
inside that Bible that gathers dust
like time on your bookshelf
and you can't bring yourself to open it
not even for a poem   not even for the grief
of love you couldn't express to him   because
above all else you fear that God will spill
out of the pages and crush you
between his flat prayer hands like a gravity
you've never even felt before   splitting
you in half and damning you to the
weight and the weight of the world

what are you doing

I want you to see that at least you *are* alive enough
to feel the days get heavier
at least you are alive enough to feel the days get heavier

and when the pressure feels persuasive chant this:
        the high gravity days don't really exist
        the high gravity days don't really exist

and every time you stress about the down
even before you've gone up
        remember the rope you tie around your waist
cannot (cannot!) be a metaphor for religion
        you have to (have to!) make it a metaphor for
yourself   otherwise, no one else will catch you
when you fall

Maddie Rae
Bellingham, Washington

Prefect

> God grant me the serenity
to accept the above misspelling
> and settle myself down
onto a comfy spot in this little universe and know
> that my right knee will hurt every day
though I admit some days less than others
> and my teenage grandson won't talk
with me like he did at ten but there's still
> that sweet conversation while we walked
down to the river to drink our smoothies
> and my son drinks beer every night
a lot
> but lately we've sort of lowered our foils,
less riposte, more touché,
> and of course I'm still racking up the rejection slips
but I have a gut feeling about this one
> and my sweetie has totally given up on sex
although hugs are still table d'hôte
> and à la carte
and laughs, God, never give up on laughs,
> we are eighteen when I can make her laugh,
so all this serenity, acceptance, whatever
> maybe even call it
pig-headedness, alls I'm asking
> is one sublime vision, veritas,
see this funky little universe never just right
> but always perfect.

Bill Griffin
Elkin, North Carolina

How to Paint a Bedroom

The painter said, you need to learn
something about technique
about how to avoid
the messes you're always getting yourself into—
the sags of paint running down your walls,
the darker color always bleeding through,
(*Little Red Riding Hood's Cape* is not the best choice, my dear,
for a southern-lit bedroom. You want a cooler color—
perhaps *Blue Bird Morning, Wings of Pegasus,* or *September Aster,*
something with less heat, less passion, he said).
And, here's another thing:
You can't just open a can of paint
and haphazardly slop it onto the walls.
You need to learn
that every can of paint is composed of its own nature
and every brush has its own personality.
Eggshell is not high gloss
and natural hair is not the same as synthetic.
There are consequences
to making such assumptions. You must learn
to mask, to cut-in, to cross coat, to feather.
You must learn patience, to let the wall breathe
and cure before painting another coat.
Maybe then, if you've been careful enough,
you will have a masterpiece. You will have learned
how to avoid curtains of *Blue Bird Morning* running down the walls
like permanently unchecked azure streams. You will have learned
to avoid hollowed out fish-eye craters pooling in the corners,
the crow's feet etching down from the ceiling like unintended
    consequences.
You will have learned something about discipline.

Stephanie A. Marcellus
Wayne, Nebraska

The Bear

When you are six, a dead bear looks like a mountain—
dark and scary up close—and if you had to climb it,
you wouldn't—you'd be too afraid. And even if you saw it
from further away, from the edge of the woods,
you might still feel a warm trickle run down your leg,
yellowing the white cuff of your sock. Mother said
to stay away, stay back at least, but you can't move
as your feet are planted, entwined with the roots
of the birch beside you, and you are just another tree,
watching. Grandpa comes, coiled rope swung
over his shoulder. Flies buzz over the stinking mountain,
and your tummy feels like it did at the fair last month,
after Mother told you too late not to ride the Tilt-O-Wheel.
Dad and Uncle wrestle the rope under the bear's neck,
their fingers swallowed by the thick black fur. They grunt
and swear at the *goddamn heavy sonofabitch*, they pull,
tug, the noose tightens, but the bear doesn't budge.
Dad hollers, Grandma hurries to the cabin to get the keys
to the old Ford flatbed. The men tie the rope's free end
to the hitch, Grandpa revs the engine. Ever so slowly,
he hauls that bear away who knows where, leaving
only a smear of blood along a trail of bent underbrush.
And I, now being a tree, stay awhile in that woodsy lot—
me and the birches have some thinking to do. Who knew
the things that scare us could be disappeared? Well, maybe
the birches did. They are probably older than me, and know more
about how stories begin and end. I am only on page 6.

Ann Weil
Ann Arbor, Michigan

Harvest

This morning, I
lost my liver, I
missed it dearly, so I
asked the man with eyes of
brown and blue if he knew where
my liver rests,
           he looks at me as if I
were dumb, and ignores
my plea but behind him there's
a tree sporting
an oozing burnt umber organ
lingering
in the heights of its limbs. I
try to scale its blotchy bark, it kept
breaking off and
crumbling in my hands, I
chase the same man, turn him around and now he
looks like a frog, his chin drooping like dew, his
green and grey eyes, he
slowly puts his hand on me, it's
moist and murky and reassuring, he
raises his other hand and
points to the fruit of the tree, bulbous electric
peach, he
reaches for it, plucks it, a
plopping sound echoing in my
bones, with vigor he
shoves it in my
liver's absence, it
           hurts, but then it
doesn't, I'm
afraid, it
glows and grows in the
pink pocket, its
fuzzy skin becomes
my fuzzy skin, its
flesh brushes against my
blushing stomach, grazes

my chittering gallbladder, then rests, I
feel queasy, I
quiver, I
lay and look above and
wonder if the tree likes my sopping liver

if it's a gift
worth giving.

C.G. Dahlin
Spokane, Washington

The Mathematician in the Henhouse

She reluctantly admits—
despite their imperfection
as three-dimensional ellipses,
the eggs soothe her palms,
and her eyes, too, with tints—
pale blue for the Araucanas,
pink from Mottled Javas
and Buff Orpingtons,
delicious chocolate brown
from the French Marans,
linen white from Leghorns.
She's put the names, breeds,
cold-hardiness, and dispositions
in a color-coded spreadsheet.

Being alone with the hens
means entering a different
dimension, full of murmurs
and sudden cackles, feathers
ornamenting nests and walls,
floors speckled with spiral galaxies
of dung. Ammonia stings
the nose and back of the tongue.

One hen's her favorite—
she has a misshapen beak
that needs some special food
and care, but the mathematician
admires the bird's friendliness—
or so it seems—always circling
toward proximity, a Fibonacci curl.

The hens feast abundantly
on the yard's cylindrical worms.
Their yolks are flawless
orange hemispheres.
What delicate dinner
will her engineer husband build

for her when he cracks
the calcareous shells,
dimpled like a baby?

Karen Kilcup
Lee, New Hampshire

Ivy

The porch I do not have smells of misandry and wine,
days-old sun-spanked sangria. I've almost carved
my place, or rather found a space that feels
not *not* my place. The questionnaire reveals
I have depression, which leaves me gray and starved
for certainty. Squirrels run the telephone line

from this balcony, third floor, where pollen collects
on the table's surface. The neighbor's wickerwork
is limp with rain, the empty painted pots
are cracked, the heavy limbs of trees in knots,
their yellowed leaves like whistling husks. I shirk
all tasks. I want the sun, as it neglects

to slice my seat of Earth, where tomatoes bow
their seedy heads. Cigarettes wave their ash-
tipped thumbs. The neighbor swings away the morning
in her rainbow hammock, thick ivy stringing
its way through a slatted wooden trellis, slash-
ing the sky like it won't get stuck right here, right now.

Christian Paulisich
Baltimore, Maryland

Autobiography of an Amnesiac

the first time I faked my death
I was reborn at a fig farm in the heart of Mexico,
eating the fruit off the tree branches
until the juice dyed my teeth
and my stomach was swollen as the moon.
we had a deal, the farmer and I.
he'd turn a blind eye to my life among his plants
and I'd eat the overripe figs, not good for selling.
every fig has a dead wasp in it.
on my fourth day I bit into my my meal and the bug,
still very much alive,
flew at me with the ferocity of an animal much larger than she was.
an hour later I was dead again and on a train to Salt Lake City,
opposite a pregnant woman weeping
and a businessman edging closer to the end of his seat with every
    wail,
her tears offending his conservative ears and his concentration on
    the business section of the
New York Times.
I give the woman a flower stomped on by dirty boots; her
    bewilderment is loud enough to stop
her crying and push me out of my seat.
I offer the man my last fig before I hurry down the aisle, imagining
    a wasp for every man, a
perpetual buzz in his ear, a constant stinging/singing until he cries
    for mercy.
one thing you learn about being a ghost is that you are a wasp,
    singing in the ears of the
unlistenting until they too are turned wanderer.

Chloe Vigil
Seattle, Washington

I Fit My Life into a Small Suitcase

—*Tatiana Bolidanova, April 19, 2022,* New York Times *quote*

What can else can be inside?
— the familiar comfort of clean socks
or a flash drive in case the cloud can't be found
& papers that may tumble into a puddle and then
you're left without proof of who you are
or where you're from in a foreign
land & can a suitcase hold the smell of boiling
food that swept the hall each evening
or dust motes swirling as you pulled
the curtain open to welcome a beginning
flowering with possibilities like bells
ringing a note that floats above rooftops
and who knows what endings
fall like loose pages edged
with stiffened glue & crumpled
with pencil marks and ink that you
rub & rub
& spit & rub again.

Aileen Bassis
Long Island City, New York

Nevermind the Years

Walk me through it again: You're standing
on a plot of Tennessee land, in the middle

of a fallow field of sunflowers whose heads
are still decaying, open wounds to the birds,

when a molten meteor or supersonic plane
skims the curve of the earth and suddenly:

You think of me. Just sitting here in Texas's
midnight quiet when your phone sings to my

phone — "Miss you when I think of you. So
I mostly don't think of you." It's all sugar; no

fangs. I think about that plane, the meteorite
ditched under half an inch of red-clay subsoil.

And if that's the kind of chase you want. If you
like it like that — red-hot, then iron-oxide tears

at the chapped-lip corners of both our hungry
mouths: interlocked, half-hearted, exhausted.

[jp/p]
Texas

Before the Cul De Sac

Timothy grass, taller than a toddler's head
teemed, all summer, wet, uninterrupted
until the hornbeam. Splintered horse fence. Moms
packed strawberries & sweet milk with XO
notes sketched into Scott napkins. At night we
gathered inside it with flashlights. Wind sliced
& groups became armies of fireflies
hunting each other in the sighing dark.
Bare legs tickled. Mouths closed, lights flew up
on stern, young faces. No one saw who threw
the brick. Even cicadas' cries paused &
we grew tall as the grass became a bed
that swallowed empties, blades, pregnancy tests,
& our bodies, strewn inside its fragrant den.

Alexander Duringer
Raleigh, North Carolina

Life remorseless

In the five weeks we were away
the wisteria snaked up the downspout
to check out the view from the rooftop
and those woody vines that refuse to be uprooted
crept through the cracks in the deck, shyly
at first, like new kids in the playground.

At first it seemed we had killed
the water kefir we left in the freezer—superannuated mush
in a plastic bag—but we jump started it
with a jolt of molasses and soon it was fizzing, as keen to live
as our granddaughter, who burst rambunctiously,
right on time, from my daughter-in-law's womb.

Sometime during this unremitting frenzy, my brother
was readmitted to hospital. Having decided to experiment
with not eating, he curled up on the threadbare carpet
and waited—*How long? Days?*—for his carer to find him.
The carer assumed that the 'caree' had fallen but, in reality,
my brother had only lain down in search of new vistas,

a new angle on the world, an ear to the floor
enabling him to better apprehend the comings and goings
of dust mites, roaches and other roommates that might have
new knowledge to impart. Needless to say,
he was picked up and packed off to hospital
where he lay for ten days on a drip, the life seeping back in,

relentless as the fussing of bees on lavender
in my rampant garden.

John Richard Heath
Washington, D.C.

Sidewalks

All I remember
about New York are
        the sidewalks

Lopsided like the world
was falling beneath
        a part_____of us

they reached to the sky
like a refusal my bike
        limping over

them now every house
with green shutters holds
        my childhood

like the shadows
that played tricks on
        my brother's eyes

making dinosaurs out
of walls and ghosts out of
        hallways

everything is bigger
on the inside
        of our ears

but we were not people
then only the sound of
        rewinding tape

on the VHS in the little
red camaro, our players
        not smart enough yet

to respond to touch
analog wonder
        made our dreams

determined and intimate
with pavement
        like my knees

and a neighbor's bandaids

Oz Paszkiewicz
Spartanburg, South Carolina

Help

A Lithuanian researcher at the med school
whom I was in love with,
Tells me *tinnitus* or "ringing in the ears,"
may sound like crashing waves,
or a million hysterical crickets,
even a chain-saw screeching of brakes.
It is found in traumatized war veterans,
and 13 million other luckless humans
leaning toward deafness—
a "ghost" sound generated by
touch-sensitive neurons to compensate
for the loss of real sound. But she
tells me this physiological help
can drive a person insane.

I tell the researcher the neurons
show us once more the often
ironic fate of good intentions.
She is lovely and inaccessible,
dedicated to relieving suffering.
Lithuania lost the highest percentage
of its population during World War II,
so she can only stare at me
like I am the insane one.
And perhaps she is right, and
my loneliness assured.
Silence moves between us like a continent.
All I have left is to await sounds
detectable only to me,
not waves, crickets, or brakes this time,
but the hopeless help of caring neurons
saying that she loves me.

Peter Stine
Berkeley, California

False Indigo

Baptisa, a prairie wildflower

Perennial like sin
Uttering underground
its own webbing
Long awaited spikes
Grown for dyeing
Wildly propagating
Through winter
To flower in spring.

This rooted framing
Ensnares my heart
Without my knowledge
Or scrutiny
It too spikes to stain
Coarsely in what seems like beauty
For its brief pleasure

But hoarfrost
blackens seed pods
with sin's dull fruit

Mary Marie Dixon
Hastings, Nebraska

Betty

People say, it's like having a baby—please! Babies stay put,
drink milk, wear diapers. *You* run loose, eat rocks, can't hold it!
Here you are chewing toes, me shouting, *stop, that hurts, no*!
Here we are, staggering by moonlight, me beside myself, you
traipsing after a hose. Goddamnit, little dog, *go*!

What's time to a puppy? A feather, a shadow, a frisky Santa Ana
wind. I'm forced to sit tight while the moon shines and you tick
around sniffing, head-butting, startled by a flicking moth,
intoxicated by jasmine, chickweed, dirt. I haven't felt this tired
since I *had* a baby, so eternally on alert!

On walks, I murmur to you like a mother, proud of my power
to steer you past danger. *It's only a trash truck, a lawnmower.*
Without me, you could swallow poison, chase cars, lose an eye.
Trusting as you are, you might follow home any stranger who
stopped to gush, *what a precious little girl—or guy?*

No baby does what you've done to my arms, or toys, or erupts in
sloppy joy then studies me like a therapist. Privately, to you alone,
I confess. I *love* you, but for goddsake! I'm over accidents, sick of
wreckage, you wild-eyed wretch! I'm inept, no match for you—
ten weeks old and smaller than a bag of chips!

We bark, face off, cuddle. I'm moved to tears by your scrap ears and
happy ignorance of plagues, wars, anytime-now apocalypse. I'm jealous!
Every night, as I load you in your crate—defeated, no, *finished*—
I hear you practically purring, nuzzling your blanket and ripped baboon,
lit by a giddy moon, as if this day, like all days, has been perfect.

Susan Heeger
Los Angeles, California

Cooling

I lived through cancer and climbed
ice-covered mountains doing it.
Like my axe piercing deep into
ice translucent blue, crystalline
and anchored, I sank into you.

I sought after and opened myself
to love like a glacier of folly,
recklessly and repeatedly,
foolishly and fully, ignoring the
layer of sugar snow, the imminence
of the avalanche on its way.

Sometimes I think I made too much
of things, conjured flawed comparisons
and monumental clichés, saw things
that weren't there, all the while
whining and whimpering,
I can get over cancer but not you.

But these were no hypothermic
delusions. I remember the
pulse of your breath and mine,
tasting of raspberry liqueur,
reading *The Dead and the Living*
softly aloud. I will never forget
how you melted into me on
that early October night, while,
across the room like an aurora,
danced a blue shimmering light.

Allison V. Craig
Albany, New York

The Catawba

At dusk
the sky opens
and the river quickens,
as if carrying
an urgent message
to the sea.
I listen for meaning
but only hear sound
and wonder
How long until this moment
reaches the ocean?
Soon night
swallows the Catawba.
I listen closely
to separate its churning
from the crickets and cars:
an endless lullaby
flowing at the speed
of time.

Isaac Rankin
Charlotte, North Carolina

The Awful Rowing

Want is irrelevant.
Need is irrelevant, too,

real but really,
beside the point.

Just letters, letters and the patterns
that sew them into sense.

These riches, past measure, everywhere,
implying a benefactor—

for the unbelieving that way suffering,
the painful-confusion-unto-despair, lies.

So, let it go, let go the giver
your little nerve-system conjures.

Concentrate, with ferocious attention,
on the gifts.

Maria Berardi
Fort Collins, Colorado

Be Doves

Violet,
be vesperal,
be twilight,

spill onto the water,
skim across the water—
dark river,

rolling rumor
scurrying
with blue-white light.

Scatter,
be scared,
be purple pulses,

airy orbs,
be bodies barely,
plump.

Breathe,
be doves,
be lathery and lift,

be feathery and fly
and find the high,
tender leaves,

quiver there,
close an eye
and roost,

be plenty there,
be plums there,
be each a pouch of prayer,

be chants,
spheres of song,
proven charms

holding back the onyx-iron,
the search and yearn
of storm, the churn and fall,

the wail, the ruptured why
at all the nothing there.
Just sky.

Kelli Logan Rush
Winston-Salem, North Carolina

That summer

lava streets swam past blank-eyed buildings,
victims of hard booted winter,
the sheen of violent winds plastered across their mouths.

Broken workers crawled away from the Caterpillar plant,
pink slips tucked between their legs.

In the fields around the dying Illinois town,
the manufactured yellow beasts belched and fell silent.

We children sucked Jolly Ranchers and popped tar bubbles
on the empty two lane road that had carried the combines
and tractors from Peoria to more prosperous farms than ours.

We stared dully at the cows. The cows stared dully
at the brown grass.

At night, with the fireflies giving them light for free,
our parents tried to touch the stars.
Their Marlboros burned their fingers.
Scars glowed red with the memory of Cadillac days.

We children couldn't sleep. We counted our ribs
and whispered secrets to the sticky night air.

AV Rasmussen
Columbus, Mississippi

Harmless Components

Living in dirt, leaving in dirt
the five percent of weapons
that don't explode. In dirt
loving each other, quickly

planting perennial species
with altered DNA. In dirt
the toxins break apart,
unlike specious arguments

online, seeded over Zoom,
grafted onto servers, safe
keeping for the creeping
rootstalks, which we are

and have always been.
We generate new shoots,
push ourselves from dirt,
away from earth, away

from what degrades
our fragile reasoning.
We send our worst
crooked philosophies

upward, to the cloud,
and that which fails
to detonate, percolates
from shells, underground.

Thomas Mixon
Sunapee, New Hampshire

Close Calls

Sun at high noon, I've parked
in the only shady spot outside
a dentist's office. Across this

heavy-trafficked street, a man
in short pants clutches a phone,
paces rapidly up and down

his driveway, protesting about
a botched repair (of what exactly
I can't discern) but manages

a forty-minute harangue to some
unfortunate worker or answering
machine. Through an open window

I hear the dentist begin to drill
just as a woman, phone in hand
marches toward my car, looks

like a cop asking me to move, but
abruptly raises her voice, turns
around as if to say, *Who cares?*

and continues to shout at someone
else. A passing bus grunts exhaust
obliging her to step on the sidewalk.

The guy across the street is still guffing.
I grab a phone to record these busy
workers, their jobs various, delicious.

Yes, America is singing, each in their
own voice, loud, vulgar, self-important,
at work dealing with most urgent matters,

but where, Walt Whitman, is the music?

Peter Neil Carroll
Belmont, California

Baseball Practice at Nichols Park

The man hopped the fence & hightailed it
across the outfield's uncut grass
as we laced up our cleats in the dugout—

the one on the first base side
which had nearly been reduced
to cinder & smoke
by a garbage fire in the winter—

face slovenly & hands caked
with fresh mud & dried blood,
his clothes, soot-stained & threadbare,
flowing behind him as a cop followed in pursuit,

biting at his ankles
like a frothy-mouthed rottweiler
chasing pickers out of a junkyard.

The man made it over the right-field fence
before the taser tagged him & sent him to the ground,
his limbs spasming & seizing
in a hundred different directions at once
until his eyes rolled up into his skull & he went limp
& belly up, like a telephoned catfish in a backwoods creek.

The cop had him handcuffed & standing
by the time our spikes were hitting the field,
had him hauled back to his cruiser
by the time we finished jogging our first pole.

Brayden Jones
Springfield, Missouri

Ode to Saran Wrap

Maybe all good things come from accidents—
a college student in a lab in Michigan,

struggling to wash out the residue of a failed
experiment, finding in that stubborn filth,

a beaker full of something else:
Polyvinylidene chloride, PVDC—

first a green spray to protect fighter jets,
then mesh insoles in combat boots

and finally, after the War, the thin,
transparent, clinging plastic wrap

we know and love. And like all
good things made by men,

it was named after a wife, Sarah,
and a daughter, Anne: a twentieth-century

mashup for the ages.
I was never really into Chemistry—

maybe it seemed too finicky or perhaps
like too much of a ministry.

I preferred physics and biology,
though abandoned both in college.

I didn't want to spend my life in a lab.
But now, there is little else more joyful

than knowing that that last little piece
of ginger can be stowed away,

as if in a cobweb that will keep it
moist and fresh, its yellow flesh

resting like a miniature sun on top of
the mayo in the refrigerator door.

The evening news is a lab report,
as oil spills in the Gulf of Mexico,

across the Dakota plains,
pickles ferment in jars on a shelf

in the foyer. I wonder what accidental
discoveries might have washed over me

in a lab coat. What would I have
named them—and after whom?

Genevieve Creedon
Bloomington, Indiana

Of Use

In his 90s, dad contributes
the good silverware
to our garage sale.
Mom's dead
and he never uses it.
Did we ever use it?

For two days we sell glasses,
a picture, and assorted junk.
The silverware case
unsold.
We lower the price.
A lot.
No sale.

Dad takes it back—
it sits in his storage cage
at the retirement community,
a sad life, even for forks,
knives, and spoons.
Shining
in a dark box.

Kenneth Pobo
Media, Pennsylvania

Poem for Silence

for Tito

When he said he wanted to be
shocked by silence, a slight window
opened where I could imagine
the blaze of quietude, how it might
amplify like rain wetting the world
all over, a different space where I might
briefly move as a dolphin, seamless
and speeding. Or the way a wet surface
grows wetter and darker—it takes
the water in until you can't imagine
how or what could be reborn though
it keeps happening, water transpiring
like tears rising and then falling,
the earth greening and whitening.
The color of the winter grasses in New Mexico,
so dry and bone-gold you could not
imagine how they would return but
each year they did with no noise
about it.

Sheila Black
San Antonio, Texas

The Second Time I Hit a Deer

was on Highway 12, late, and she
torpedoed into my truck
like a bird.

And there were those seconds
before it happened but after
I knew it was happening

when I felt so little, except
purpose, and try. Try
to make it not happen. Try

to dodge with your body, your
own body, stationary in motion, as if
the body of the uncaring truck will mirror

your flinch, your try. And when it
doesn't work, try
to feel more than chagrin
at the insurance

claim yet to be claimed, try.

Kate Nootenboom
Johnstown, Nebraska

That Kind of Summer

Carved jade locusts. Seventeen-year antiquities.
Locusts big as mockingbirds. In shiny green
raincoats. Sing Puccini and Verde. Discard
jackets on porch rail and window ledge.
Chew tree and shrub to lace. Hibiscus bells
ring from green lattice.

Mockingbirds big as flamingos. Kick-the-can
in the street. Flash petticoats
like can-can dancers. Mockingbirds gone mute.
Not a single bridge or riff of plagiarized song.
Mockingbirds struck dumb by locusts.

A young girl gathers dandelions. Breathes—
a hundred ballerinas pirouette the air.
Above locusts. Above mockingbirds. The girl
is a spirit drum. Chain of dandelions in her hair.
Her bare feet pound bare earth. Bass line.

Sun, ragged dandelion, spreads iridescence.
Girl's sky-dye shift. Sky blue day.
Mockingbirds, bellies filled with locusts,
tumble from trees. It's that kind of summer.

Ann Howells
Carrollton, Texas

First Mammal at Continent's Edge

What if today I were felled
by a drive-by bullet,
flattened by a falling tree?
Shouldn't I think of all I'd miss,
who I'd never touch again,
everything left unfinished
instead of the "To Do"

list on my desk,
its reminders about baby wipes,
a flea collar, unclogging a drain,
a note to buy mascara
to look like a badass,
the list jotted sipping coffee to jolt
me from last night's dream
about driving an Appian Way
narrowing to rubble,
walking over rocks barefoot
to reach the sea,
the first mammal roaming
a continent's edge?

I rush home from Pilates
to hide the list
before it's seen,
hoping today is not the day
I'm hit by a truck while
picturing a post-it with return calls
to accept a laureate,
an interview with David Remnick,
plans to windsail the Sahara.

Lily Jarman-Reisch
Baltimore, Maryland

I Recently Learned

to put one foot in front of the other without collapsing
to see you sullen-mouthed and grinning all at once

the absence of reflux feels like a presence
the damp tissue in my hand makes me itch behind the ears

wherever we are, a spider is watching, scared, soon to be eaten by its
    children
wherever the cosmos pulses pink/yellow/blue in black space-sky

I am the prevaricating precariat wire-walking between imaginary
    skyscrapers
I am the unintended ransom note wrapped in a riddle of
    consecrated consequences

nothing came first; everything took forever
nothing I worried about was accurate or holy

it is already over.

Julie Benesh
Chicago, Illinois

Heavy Under the Heart

I sit in the glider, child in my arms
wrapped tight in his blanket, hands
pinned to his sides, happy this way:

no decisions to make
or wish unmade.

I rock him back and forth, feet up
on the rest. The weight on my chest
good ballast, solid presence, answer
("I refute him thus") to sceptic Berkeley,

firm and down-pressing like a curled-up
cat, a sleeping dog, a beloved
head. Warm as a loaf of bread
just pulled from the oven on a long
wooden peel, cherry pie steaming
on a sill. The days to come seem
far away when we'll yell at him
about his grades, and worry when
he doesn't call.

Grandma Yetta warned my dad
don't eat cherries right before bed.
"Cherries lie heavy under the heart,"
she said. Little baldy, little plum,
more than worth your weight in
indigestion, I hold you fast
as a diver grasps the stone that
carries him away to the bottom.

Julian Koslow
Fair Lawn, New Jersey

I Named You for Her

When you first were wrenched out
of my cut-open stomach, you passed
the pile of neatly stacked organs

they had taken out of me to reach
you lined up around the wound
and I wanted to die. *You'll feel*

a little tugging now, the Dr. said
and I wanted to scream, *You started
without me?* You, neck noosed

twice by the umbilical cord, blue
face and toes. I heard them talk
as I was sewn up, and then you

cried, a long peal of protest against
air, against light, against being one
and alone. Against. Against. Again.

Until they put you on my chest, blind
eyes, sniffing. Lips finding my nipple
and the sudden tough tug release sniff

tug release sniff not a sound
as the other breast squirted out
a geyser of milk. The nurse, eaglet

young, laughed and lifted you
and put you on the second breast.
I wanted to die. I knew nothing. No.

Thing. Until my grandmother, dead
these 18 years, came through
the wall to sit by my side.

Gunilla T. Kester
Williamsville, New York

Heat Maps

Yesterday, 192 million birds
left their homes
for safer weather
and I sat on my porch
sipping coffee torn
from their summer hillsides
meanwhile, my friend
machines precision parts
for missiles
headed to Ukraine!
so proudly put
and I wonder if yesterday,
or the day before that,
they migrated themselves
to some other country
dictator or democracy
forcing movement
around the globe
the sound of fleeing feet
no better atmosphere
I wonder, too, if birds scan
the skies above
with feathered Doppler maps
beaks poised prow-like,
flocks of piercing questions

Ann Fisher
Lincoln, Vermont

Seal of Delight

I'm doing my slow
old-lady jog,
earbuds in so I can listen
to Ross Gay's delight,
when I hear a splash
and see a harbor seal
shoot out of Elliott Bay,
a vertical, smooth
black cylinder of joy—
okay, maybe it is just
a seal trying to catch a fish
but it looks like joy to me—
and I decide
I'll go with that,
this will do:
the seal surfaces,
leaps, huffs,
a wet splash
of body, tail, flippers,
then one last
thrust of muscle
up and up, and I swear
the seal laughs
while yellow kelp
trails from her mouth
and a million tiny
droplets of sea water
cascade like silver sparks
from a risen god.

Cindy Buchanan
Seattle, Washington

Wilkens Farm

Your eyes scan a field dotted with haystacks,
over-ripe pumpkins, and the lazy buzz of saturated bees
sleepwalking their way towards death.

I tilt my face skywards at the faded sun
and count back thirteen years: It's July
and your braces are finally off.

The sun stands strong above our heads,
and the grass is bright. Green is still green
and not yet an allegory for jealousy or greed.

I anticipate the ice cream man
who comes at three and the slow curve of sky
unrolling around the horizon.

You run your tongue over the smooth, clean
surface of your newly unbent teeth,
relishing their glossiness.

Today we watch the apple trees deplete,
leaves whirling to earth in a slow curdle,
wondering, will we ever feel that limitless again?

Chelsea Fanning
Jersey City, New Jersey

Shopkeeper

a dream for Ted Kooser

You set up shop under a shade tree,
pour apple cider for the kids, line up

well-worn shoes and tools—the nuts
and bolts of dailiness. You seem to be

at the mouth of a cave, its breath cooling,
halfway between darkness and sun.

Your table, an old door across sawhorses,
and everyone knows a poem is a door

hung between worlds, a web strung
to rescue the heart as it squirms for mercy.

I can't tell if you're selling or giving
your wares away—less my father gladhanding

at sales conventions, more like your own
at the counter, unspooling bolts of drapery

cloth, the sheen a hum beneath his hands.
Everyone knows the same entrance calls us,

echoing the long gone, the threshold planed
with comings and goings. Sometimes we fall

back, sometimes lean forward, either way
a mystery. Whatever bargain this poem is,

you've dusted it off, you've smiled kindly,
you've traded it for a Yankee dime (a peck

on the cheek), the deep night at arm's length
behind you.

Linda Parsons
Knoxville, Tennessee

The Stationary Bike

Sleek and spare, it tells on glowing
dials how long, how far, how many
calories burned. Four bars of tension
for the pulse, then six, then a wild
ten as the heart settles, finds its pace.

Nothing much moves as I pedal
weightless on worn knees, pumping
past a granddaughter's 29th birthday,
past my father's birth a century ago,
through Thanksgiving, 40 years of
marriage, months of pandemic fading
in the rear-view mirror I do not have.

Zooming through poetry readings,
workshops, contests, a class on the
neglected Apocrypha, board meetings
that creep into one's solitude,
                                      masking
for groceries, wine, gin, beer, brandy,
a daring foray into outdoor dining
before winter settles in,
                              long distance calls,
cross-continent Facetime with grandkids
doing cartwheels, headstands as we chat,
unbelievably tall across months we have
not touched.
                          Sweatshirt damp, heart
surging—ten miles, 240 calories, the slim
slice of pecan pie I topped off lunch with—
I dismount, get shaky legs under me,
head toward a shower, email, Chinese
take-out for dinner, decisions about
*Masterpiece, The Office, Death in
Paradise* during another evening,

toward Facebook condolences for
a friend dead far too young, news about

crowded hospitals, spiking numbers,
old people lonely in their rooms, a vaccine
like a pace rabbit we pedal toward,
furiously, in place.

Harry Moore
Decatur, Alabama

Field Book of Common Rocks and Minerals

Kansas is silt and silica,
limestone, loess, a trace

of lead, the faint thumbprints
of glaciers in its sediment and shale.

Chalcedony occurs in cavities,
coats surfaces and seams. Chipped

into rudimentary tools and spears,
it cemented man's dominion.

Jasper, heavy with hematite,
is opaque and red as blood that beads

along an edge of scab. When
the Jasper Room in Russia's

Winter Palace burned, it returned
as the Malachite Drawing Room.

Picture it! This copper carbonate,
its vivid green unmistakable, adamantine,

culled from the Urals and cut into columns,
urns, and hearths, this room now rich

as rain forest, impressive as cities
of emerald. Here Empresses dressed

their daughters, the Romanov brides,
in satin trains with stitches fine as grains

of sand, to process past pillars
Eden green and into the Tsar's

Grand Church. Until the last—
Alexandra—whose own daughters

died motherless, childless,
executed with copper, lead, and steel.

Terry Hall Bodine
Lynchburg, Virginia

Sophocles' Sonnet

And who is it that rides the sea as conqueror
But Man, the Earth's great wonder, miracle and prize,
And kisses Earth, caresses her yet ploughs on her
Again as conqueror and king, and Moon he eyes
Above to make his own one day, and then the stars.
He's lion, eagle, stallion, aurochs all in one.
His art's immortal; then it's only Death that bars
The way to join him with his art's transcendent run
Down all the roads and trails of time. He raises law
And then betrays his law on whim, as gods betray
Their laws upon some higher purpose—or a whim.
In rock-strong buildings to the clouds he mocks what's raw
In nature's weather; ever seeks some higher way
Of being; pours until his wine has crossed the brim.

Ira Rosenstein
Long Island City, New York

Imagine Wearing This

I bought a mail-order coffee-colored velvet peacoat.
A bright lime and yellow jacket, the weave frayed open

at the cuffs. I bought a coat dress, double-breasted, notched
lapels, made from boysenberry worsted wool. Its skirt

was hemmed precipitously, perilously, to several inches
higher than my knee. The palate wants what it has tasted,

and it tastes what the family can afford to place upon the table.
I was nineteen or twenty. My mother saw me off that morning,

she handed me my bag and then she leaned against the door
frame, waving in her faded duster while I drove away. It was a long,

long elevator ride, the first and only time I wore the purple dress.
The doors slid soundlessly apart, delivered me into a flock

of four or five sea island cotton-wearing men in muted tones.
They flushed and coughed; they stepped aside to make a cavity

and I spilled in, my sweet and sticky pulp. For thirty floors
I was reflected in the mirrored panels, the rows of buttons

sewn a little crooked on their threads. The wool was rough,
the color, lurid. Like a juice that stains the skins it touches.

Jennifer A Sutherland
Baltimore, Maryland

Something about Eighteen and Goose Lake Festival Where I Saw the Flying Burrito Brothers Play

Dreaming of ten thousand places
we weren't supposed to be, we became jumpers
of wire fences, fooling soft equivalents
of the Hell's Angels when we rode
the mesh and dropped over the top.
I looked at the pot-bellied long hairs
in motorcycle jackets, bandaged bruises
wanting to be free of bad skin but not this weekend.
With thick-maned hair we wandered
a year after Woodstock, through the cropped crowd,
who sprawled on beach blankets
in a pasture of blistering heat.

We had left the planet, one with wire
protecting us from such scenes, and I saw Gram Parsons
alive as he could be, up on stage wearing
his nudie duds with the Flying Burrito Brothers,
whose pencil-thin mustache was barely grown in.
This old town is filled with sin,
Gram sang to the crowd, waving his hips
like hands at the sunburned faces of girls, whose
pill taking would keep them from making thirty;
on guitar his man played pedal steel, unburdening a sound
like streams of wire waving end on end.

We were jumpers with fences inside us, too.
Like Gram who couldn't find a last handhold
to pull him free before so many stars settled in his lungs.
We strolled past fences that kept us
contained like cattle, some with blown bits
of newspaper, or other daylong debris.
We assembled in lines for outhouse troughs,
a part of the dreaming people, who had come
for what could no longer be explained, saw stars
at night like those drafted soldiers who never

escaped their bloody fate in Vietnam to dream
of other places they had never been at eighteen.

Russell Thorburn
Marquette, Michigan

The Mother Part

Before breakfast: my fingers
fumbling the small pill
inside me. I bleed

on the tile. Empty
out. Outside, all the buildings
pitted with pink windows.

The hollow spot
in the sink where sometimes
the cat cleans herself,

the tender grit
of her pink tongue.
When I was young,

another cat crawled under
my bed to deliver. I thought
she was dying

& after, watched her
eat her newborn, still-gray
& clot-wet. I watched her clean

the mess, & then a hole appeared
like a stone in my stomach.
Things are emptied

all the time. My mother
once told me
every woman carries

a secret. I'll never tell her,
so I guess this is mine:
a hole in the mother

part of me. It's ok,
pit the fruit's wet-flesh.
Cleave the seed

soft as tissue
from tissue. Surely, I am
not the only one.

Chloe Forsell
Brooklyn, New York

Fable

Coyotes sleep nose to tail in dank caves. A lonesome
mountain lion lids the slats of her eyes. In the wind
yucca flowers dune and drift. I know the names of things
here, the very rise where my father's bones lie,
not so far from my grandfather's, and save a sad handful
of stories that's as far as we go. Like a city street
that ends in a high fence, and it is unclear what has been
fenced in, or out, and even here, in this nameless city,
you'll find coyotes snouting and slavering after grease
and trash, the odd housecat, and it's their recolonizing racket
that wakes the child, who rises, whose small hands tremble
against cold window glass, and the child's father, a man
whose daily work is to take work away from other men, leads
the child back to bed, tucks him in, blesses him, blesses him.

Joe Wilkins
McMinnville, Oregon

Your Dad's Record Collection

These worn record jackets of Ramones
and The Clash, your dad's stash of albums,

now weathered like the man, are your birthright.
Find within a black vinyl moon and slip it

from its sleeve. Hear the same hiss and crackle
that rattled him into manhood. How handsome

he stood in front of those cherry wood speakers
and lit receiver, in threadbare Levi's, long hair

past his eyes, headbanging to shock waves
of bass. These LPs are an arc from his youth

to yours, so stand before the speakers
with your turned up collar. Hear the same hiss

of artifact and artifice, that sacred pop
when the needle drops and sound explodes

a beat before Joey Ramone bleats:
I wanna be sedated.

Dawn Dupler
Ballwin, Missouri

when I type "what happens" Google suggests "when you die"

And suddenly I love everyone including
absurd little dictators and unkind

people on the internet. On the trail
in Spain two middle-aged men met.

They began to travel together.
They made friends in each town.

In the dim cafes they shared
late-afternoon café con leche.

They said *Back home we live only
two towns apart. Can you believe*

we had to cross an ocean to find each other?
Every morning they shouldered their

bags in a new courtyard, gripped the
rubber handles of their two trekking poles,

and sang out loudly but not very well:
we'll meet again / don't know where /

don't know when. They were standing
in the sun in a place no one

belonged to. Whenever I
remember them I believe them.

Bryana Joy
Bethlehem, Pennsylvania

9 789898 537806 1